131
Creative Conversations
for Couples

Christ-honoring questions to
deepen your relationship,
grow your friendship,
and kindle romance.

Jed Jurchenko

www.CoffeeShopC

© 2016 by Jed Jurchenko.

Scripture quoted by permission.
All scripture quotations,
unless otherwise indicated,
are taken from the NET Bible®
copyright ©1996-2006
by Biblical Studies Press, L.L.C.
All rights reserved.

Printed by CreateSpace,
An Amazon.com Company
Available from Amazon.com

Creative, Christ-honoring
conversation starters to grow your
relationship and deepen your connection!

Also by Jed

131 Conversations That Engage Kids

131 Boredom Busters and Creativity Builders

131 Creative Conversations for Couples

131 Engaging Conversations for Couples

131 Creative Conversations for Families

131 Necessary Conversations before Marriage

131 Conversations for Stepfamily Success

131 Connecting Conversations
for Parents and Teens

Ten Quick Wins for Writers

Coffee Shop Conversations:
Psychology and the Bible

Get Free Books

To thank you for your purchase, I would like to send you a bonus gift.

Transform from discouraged and burned out to an enthusiastic agent of joy who parents at a higher, happier level. *Be Happier Now* provides ten easy-to-apply happiness strategies for reducing stress and increasing joy at home!

I will also make sure that you are the first to know about free books and future deals!

www.coffeeshopconversations.com/happiness/

Dedication

To my wife, Jenny. Thank you for the many incredible date nights. The evenings spent sipping coffee, asking great questions, and dreaming about our future together are among my favorite memories. The fun, adventure, love, and friendship that you add to my life is astounding!

To my daughters Mackenzie, Brooklyn, Addison, and Emmalynn. You added an overwhelming amount of joy to my life, and I love each of you! Although you four are a long way away from dating and marriage, my prayer is that, when the time is right, you will experience the joy that comes from finding a best friend with whom you can share your inner world.

Contents

Introduction
The Power of Connection

Love, friendship, and romance are fundamental ingredients in a lasting relationship. While they are by no means the only factors, they are essential. A relationship lacking these qualities is like baking brownies and leaving out the chocolate, eggs, or sugar. When key components are missing, a decadent treat becomes dull and bland.

Sadly, "dull and bland" sums up far too many relationships. I remember the dean of our seminary proclaiming, "The loneliest people in America are not the single adults. They are married couples, who fall asleep— back-to-back, thinking to themselves, *when is this emptiness going to end?'"* His words are packed with truth. Single adults have the hope of meeting that special someone and living happily ever after.

Feeling trapped in a tasteless pancakes-with-no-syrup, toast-without-butter, hospital -mush relationship is depressing. The good news is that if your relationship is in a slump, it doesn't have to stay that way. Moreover, if you are one of those happy couples who are already best friends, then the questions in this book will assist you in building upon this solid foundation.

Mixing in the Key Ingredients

Love, friendship, and romance—three critical ingredients of a happy relationship—share the common thread of intimacy. My favorite definition of *intimacy* is "in-to-me-see." It is the ability to peer into the heart of another while simultaneously allowing that person to gaze into your inner world.

In an intimate relationship, two people know each other inside and out, or to use a biblical phrase, "the two become one." The intimate couple chooses to accept each other as is, warts and all. They make the intentional decision to find joy as a couple. This level of intimacy builds over time. It is the result of a mutual sharing of:

- Feelings
- Dreams

- Desires
- Fears
- Future aspirations
- Hopes
- Casual thoughts

Intimacy happens at the intersection of the casual, deep, and spiritual. From the simple knowledge of the other person's favorite meal to understanding their deep fears and connection to their Creator, intimacy covers everything.

Yet knowledge alone is not enough. Knowing is only the first step to a happy partnership. When I envision an intimate relationship, I imagine:

- A couple in their nineties, strolling hand in hand along the seashore.
- A young couple—juggling multiple jobs and a house full of kids—who long to spend every spare moment in each other's presence.
- An established couple in their fifties—settled into the routine of life—who considers their time together to be the highlight of their week.

Love is an action word. The purpose of gaining a more in-depth knowledge is to improve our acts of love. It is our daily demonstrations of love–shown through a playful, joyful friendship–that matter most. This is where intimacy leads. The destination is two people who know one another fully, care for each other deeply, and are excited about spending time in each other's presence.

Fostering Intimacy

The questions in this book are designed to foster intimacy. In the pages ahead, you will find 131 open-ended questions. This means that more than a simple yes or no answer will be required. Many questions are followed up with the question "why?" in order to mine deeper into your partner's heart.

Working through this book as a couple is a gift. It is the gift of time, the gift of knowledge, and most of all, the gift of you. Back when my wife and I began dating, I kept a similar book of questions in my car.

Jenny and I worked through each inquiry — one by one — over a number of weeks. We shared our hopes, dreams, and outlook on life. We laughed in coffee shops, chatted on dinner dates, and took turns asking questions while relaxing at the beach.

These times of mutual sharing were a highlight of our two-and-a-half years of dating. Now that we are married, Jenny and I continue to ask excellent questions. Of course, this is expected when a social worker and therapist unite.

As I researched other books on questions for couples, I noticed three primary complaints. Some books include R-rated material that was embarrassing and stirred up conflict. Others contained questions quickly answered with a simple yes or no. The result was an experience that felt more like an interrogation than an intimate connection. Finally, older couples reported that, in many cases, they already knew what their partner's reply would be. As a result, these couples breezed through the book without in-depth discussion taking place.

This book is different. Every question will stir up conversations that extend beyond what you already know. As a marriage and family therapist and seminary professor, I am good at asking questions. I packed this book with creative share-your-inner-world type of questions. Whether you are in the beginning stages of your relationship or approaching your golden anniversary, this book will lead you to deeper levels of intimacy and add value to your lives.

Getting Started

In the pages ahead, you will find 131 questions for deepening your love, friendship, and romance. There are no rules attached. My suggestion is that the two of you work through these questions one at a time over a multitude of dates.

Date ideas include:

- Picnics in the park.
- Outings to a favorite restaurant. (Try going through a question or two while waiting for your meal.)

- Keep a copy in your purse or on your smartphone. Pull it out whenever there is a lull in the conversation.
- Bring this book with you on a road trip.
- Keep a copy on your kitchen table and dive into a question over breakfast each morning.
- Ask these questions during an evening bonfire.
- Walk to a coffee shop together and work through the book while enjoying a favorite beverage.
- Arrive at a movie early and go through a few questions while you wait for the show to start.

As you work through this book, here are some connection strategies to keep in mind.

Take your time. There is nothing magical about these questions and no prize for finishing the book. The reward is in the bonding. So, by all means, slow down and enjoy the process. If the two of you find yourselves engaged in conversation, set the book down and keep talking—you are doing things right.

Turn toward your partner. This is also known as having good micro-skills. Micro-skills are the nonverbal ways that we communicate "I am interested in you." Experts estimate that anywhere from 50 to 90 percent of our communication takes place nonverbally. Thus, you will want to pay careful attention to this area. Here is a quick breakdown of essential micro-skills that will amplify your connection:

- Sit with an open posture, with arms and legs uncrossed.
- Turn your body toward your partner.
- Make steady eye contact.
- Smile.
- Ask open-ended questions that encourage discussion.
- Turn your cell phone off, and give your partner the gift of distraction-free time.

Strive for understanding. This book is not about working through long-standing issues nor getting caught up in heated disagreements. Instead, it is meant to foster an appreciation for similarities and differences and to create a greater understanding of each person's unique contribution to the relationship. Opposites attract. If you and your partner shared similar thinking in all areas, one of you wouldn't be needed. Everybody has the need to feel heard and understood. Practice validating your partner's feelings and watch your intimacy grow.

Have fun! William Glasser, the renowned therapist and founder of choice theory, listed *fun* as one of the five basic human needs. Fun is serious business. Remember, you are connecting with someone you care about deeply. So enjoy these moments to the fullest!

Some questions in this book are serious. Others lighten the mood. All of them facilitate connection.

Ecclesiastes 4:9–10 says, "Two people are better than one, because they can reap more benefit from their labor. For if they fall, one will help his companion up, but pity the person who falls down and has no one to help him up."

A couple that teams up to strengthen their love, friendship, and romance is pursuing a worthy goal. My prayer is that as you dive into these questions, the two of you develop a deeper bond than ever before!

Sincerely,

COFFEE SHOP CONVERSATIONS

131
Creative Conversations
for Couples

Ask the right questions if you're going to find the right answers.

~ Vanessa Redgrave

Counsel in a person's heart is like deep water, but an understanding person draws it out.

~ Proverbs 20:5

Question #1

Imagine that you could send a letter back in time to your younger self. What would your message say, and to which year would you address it?

Question #2

Growing up, what was one of your favorite family traditions? Describe what made this time extra special.

Question #3

Imagine that on your next birthday your rich uncle tells you his present to you is the gift of a perfect day. Then he hands you his credit card. For the next twenty-four hours, there are no limits to what you can spend. Where will you go, what will you do, and whom will you take with you?

Question #4

If you had to choose between the two, would you rather die exactly three years from today or live so long that you outlast all your friends? Why?

Question #5

Describe the most adventurous thing you have ever done. If you were given the opportunity, would you do this again?

Question #6

Describe an adventurous activity that you would like to do in the future. What makes that adventure so appealing?

Question #7

Who was your childhood best friend, and what made this relationship so special?

Question #8

Most teenagers occasionally have awkward moments. Describe an embarrassing time from your teenage years.

Question #9

Growing up, what household rule did you dislike the most, and why?

Question #10

Growing up, what household rule benefited you the most? Why was this rule helpful, and will you pass it on to your own children?

Question #11

Describe a childhood mentor, teacher, or coach who had a positive impact on your life. What was it that this person said or did that was so meaningful?

Question #12

Imagine a genie from a magic lamp grants you one life do-over. What past event would you change, and how would you do things differently?

Question #13

If you could have dinner with a present-day hero, who would it be, and why?

Question #14

If you could travel back in time and dine with any historical figure, whom would you eat with, and why?

Question #15

In your opinion, what is one mistake your parents made in raising you? How will you do things differently with your own children?

Question #16

What is one thing your parents did right in raising you? Why was this so meaningful?

Question #17

Describe a time in your life when you felt especially close to God. Why do you think you felt so close to Him during that season of life?

Question #18

What are you currently doing to nurture yourself spiritually? Are there spiritual activities you did in the past that you miss?

Love is patient, Love is kind...

~1 Corinthians 13:4

Question #19

If you had to decide between a career with money and fame—where you are away from your family over two hundred days a year—or a job where you are unknown but can return to your family at the end of the day, which would you choose, and why?

Question #20

If you could visit anywhere in the world, where would it be, and why?

Question #21

Growing up, what were some of your favorite childhood toys and television shows?

Question #22

Describe one accomplishment you are especially proud of.

Question #23

Imagine that you can peer into the future. Describe what your life looks like precisely five years from now. What career are you working? Who are your friends? What are your hobbies, and how are you spending the majority of your time?

Question #24

Now imagine that you peer even further into the future. Describe what your life looks like ten years from today.

Question #25

Would you rather be unable to have children at all, or only be able to birth quadruplets? Why?

You know you're in love when you can't fall asleep because reality is finally better than your dreams.
~Dr. Seuss

Question #26

Who is one couple you admire? What is it that makes this couple's relationship great?

Question #27

Growing up, what was it like when your parents were angry with you? What will you do differently when you become angry with your own children?

Question #28

Describe what it was like for you when your parents were angry with each other.

Question #29

What do you do when you get angry with someone you care about? Is this similar or different than your parents' style of anger? Why?

Question #30

Describe a perfect date night. What would you do? Where would you go? Whom would you take with you?

Question #31

When you are in a bad mood, what is one simple thing your partner can do to brighten your day?

Question #32

What is one book that influenced your life? How did this book help shape you and your worldview?

Question #33

In America the divorce rate is nearly 50 percent. What do you believe it takes to make a marriage last?

Question #34

Imagine that you are mentoring a troubled teen and can offer one piece of advice. What wisdom do you share?

Question #35

If you were asked to offer one piece of spiritual advice in church, what recommendation would you give? What makes this advice important to you personally?

Question #36

What do you think is the most significant quality of lasting friendships? How do you demonstrate these qualities yourself?

Question #37

Who is your best friend right now? What is it that you like most about this friend?

Question #38

In your opinion, why do so many marriages fail?

Question #39

What political party do you most closely associate with, and why?

Question #40

What spiritual beliefs are most important to you, and why?

Question #41

Imagine that you will be stranded on a deserted island for a year. You are allowed to take one personal item with you. What would you bring, and why?

Question #42

What is one food you would happily eat every day for the next year?

Question #43

What are some of life's simple pleasures that make you smile?

Question #44

What is one wrong in the world that you are passionate about changing for the better?

Question #45

If you could have one superpower, what would it be? How would you use it?

Love is like the wind,
you can't see it but you can feel it.
~Nicholas Sparks

Question #46

Imagine that you become the president of the United States for one hour and have the power to enact one law. What law would you make or change? Why?

Question #47

What Bible story or passage of Scripture is especially meaningful to you, and why?

Question #48

What is one decision you regret making, and what do you wish you had done differently?

Question #49

If you were to create a bucket list, what would your top three to five items be?

Question #50

Imagine that a rich uncle passes away. His last wish was to donate his multimillion-dollar fortune to charity. However, no charity was designated in the will, and you are asked to distribute his wealth. What charities will you donate to, and why?

Question #51

What hobby or activity do you believe will play an essential part in your life for as long as you live? Why is this activity so important to you?

Question #52

If you won a thousand dollars today, would you be more likely to take a vacation, make a purchase, pay down bills, or save it? Why?

Question #53

Do you believe there is such a thing as "good debt"? If so, what things are worth going into debt over?

Question #54

Who is the happiest person you know? What do you think makes this person so upbeat?

Question #55

Do you consider yourself a happy person? If so, what do you do to stay in a good mood? If not, what would it take to make you happy?

Question #56

If you created a list of the things you are most afraid of, what would be the top three items on this list?

Question #57

If you had to choose to go through the remainder of your life with either no arms or no legs, which would you choose, and why?

Question #58

When you were a child, how did you answer the question, "What do you want to be when you grow up?" Has your answer changed over time?

Question #59

If you could have any job in the world, what would it be, and why?

Question #60

When was the last time you felt embarrassed? Describe what happened that made you feel this way.

Question #61

When is the last time you felt happy? What made you feel this way?

Question #62

Are there any causes or people you feel so passionate about that you would be willing to die for them? If so, what or who are they?

Question #63

Imagine you find yourself standing before God and He asks, "Why should I let you into my heaven?" How would you reply?

Question #64

If you could ask God any one question, what would it be? Why?

Question #65

Imagine you have a thriving career as a therapist. Every day you meet with clients who are drug addicts, domestic-violence victims, mentally ill, or in the prison system. Are there any types of clients you would absolutely refuse to meet with? If so, who would you be unwilling to meet with, and why?

Question #66

How were you disciplined as a child? Will you discipline your own children in a similar manner? Why or why not?

Question #67

In your opinion, what is the best way to instill positive values in children?

Where there is love there is life.
~ Mahatma Gandhi

Question #68

If you could be remembered for only one thing, what would you like to be known for?

Question #69

When you find yourself sad, mad, or frustrated, is it easy or difficult to share how you are feeling with others? Why do you think talking about how you feel does or does not come naturally for you?

Question #70

Describe a time in your life when you were afraid. If you were afraid right now, how would those around you know?

Question #71

Would you rather go through life not being able to see or not being able to hear, and why?

Question #72

Which holiday is your favorite, and what is one of your most cherished holiday memories?

Question #73

Imagine that your significant other says they want to make this Valentine's Day the best ever. What would he or she do to make the day extra special?

Question #74

If you were asked to give helpful advice to a couple who is arguing continually, what would you say to them?

Question #75

How do you know if someone is trustworthy? Do you consider yourself a trustworthy person?

Question #76

Describe a favorite childhood vacation. What was it that made this getaway so special?

Question #77

If you were going through a difficult time and needed to seek out wise advice, whom would you turn to, and why?

Question #78

What are you currently doing to make this world a better place? If you cannot think of anything, what types of things would you like to do in the future?

To love at all is to be vulnerable.
~ C.S. Lewis

Question #79

Imagine you have the opportunity to listen to your own eulogy. What types of statements do you hope are being made about you?

Question #80

Who is one person you would like to model your life after? What specific qualities does this person have that you want to build into your own life?

Question #81

What do you consider to be your greatest strengths?

Question #82

What do you consider to be your most significant weaknesses?

Question #83

If you had the opportunity to give our current president one piece of advice, what suggestion would you give?

Question #84

Most everyone has at least a few "hot buttons," or little things that easily annoy them. What are some of yours?

Question #85

Do you believe that men and women should hold traditional gender roles today (such as the man being the primary "bread-winner" for the family and the woman being a homemaker and primary caregiver for the children)? Why or why not?

Love does no wrong to a neighbor.

~ Romans 13:10

Question #86

When you were growing up, did your parents follow traditional gender roles? Do you believe this had a positive or negative impact on their overall relationship?

Question #87

Every family has their own unique family culture. Describe some of the important aspects of your family's culture when you were growing up.

Question #88

Describe the type of family culture that you would ideally like to have.

Question #89

"Children should be seen and not heard." Do you agree with this statement? Why or why not?

Question #90

What types of things make a movie or television show offensive to you? Have you ever gone to a movie that was so offensive you decided to walk out?

Question #91

In your opinion, what type of activities do a spiritually healthy couple do together? Are there any spiritual activities that you would like to start doing as a couple?

Question #92

Have you ever been the victim of discrimination, bullying, or racism? If so, what happened, and how did it make you feel?

Question #93

If you had to choose a career other than the one you are currently in, what job would you pick, and why?

Question #94

Imagine you receive a call from the local zoo stating that they are closing down. All their animals—including the exotic ones—are up for adoption. Which animal or animals would you adopt, and how would you care for them?

Question #95

If you had to choose between the two, would you rather have:

A. A few close friends whom you know well.

B. Many friends with whom you have a surface-level relationship.

Why?

Question #96

If you and your partner were getting over a big fight, what is one small step that your partner could take to begin making amends?

Question #97

If your loved one wanted to do something simple to show you he or she cared, what would this look like?

Question #98

What is one religious belief your church holds that you disagree with?

Question #99

What one movie do you think everyone should see, and why?

Question #100

On a scale of one to ten, with one being not very important and ten being extremely important, how essential is your faith to you?

Question #101

How old were you when you started driving? Do you believe this is a good age for kids to learn to drive today? Why, or why not?

Question #102

If you were to pick a fictional television family you would most like your own family to resemble, which family would it be, and why?

Question #103

Describe the worst date you ever had. What made this date so bad?

Question #104

From your perspective, what does it mean for a couple to fight fair?

Question #105

In your opinion, what does it look like when a couple fights dirty?

Question #106

How would you describe your own conflict style? Is it fair, dirty, or a mixture of both?

Question #107

What is one conflict you've had that you feel was resolved well? What is it that made the conflict resolution work?

Question #108

If you could change any one thing about your physical appearance, what would it be, and why?

Question #109

In your opinion, what is one area of our relationship we could work on together to make our connection even stronger?

Question #110

If you knew you were going to die at this exact time tomorrow, how would you spend the next twenty-four hours?

Question #111

Do you believe in love at first sight? Why, or why not?

Question #112

What do you think are the most important things parents can do to raise great kids?

Question #113

What do you like best about our current relationship?

Question #114

If you learned that one week from today you would suddenly lose your ability to see, how would you spend the next week?

Question #115

If you had to choose between a career you love that pays just over minimum wage or a job you despise that will make you wealthy, which one would you pick, and why?

Question #116

Growing up, what were some of your favorite childhood stories and books?

Question #117

Imagine that you woke up one morning and discovered you had traveled back in time to the day after you graduated from high school. As you move forward and relive your life, what is one thing you would do differently? What is one thing you would do exactly the same?

Question #118

In your opinion, what is the single most critical ingredient for making a relationship work?

Question #119

How old were you when you got your first cell phone? At what age do you think it is appropriate for children to have their own phone?

Question #120

What is one life experience you had that was so amazing you would relive it again if you could?

Question #121

What has been one challenging experience in your life that has resulted in you becoming a better person? In what ways did this incident help you improve yourself?

Question #122

What is one of your favorite childhood memories with one or both of your parents? What makes this memory so meaningful to you?

Question #123

In most families, members take on a family role. There is the black sheep who is always blamed for the problems, the hero who can do no wrong, the judge who mediates to keep the peace, and the nurse who comforts those who are hurting. What image would you use to describe your role in your family as you grew up?

Question #124

How would you describe your role in your family now that you are an adult? Do you think your role has changed?

Question #125

What was your parents' attitude toward alcohol growing up? In what ways is your attitude toward alcohol the same as or different from that of your parents?

Question #126

Would you describe your life as easy, average, or exceptionally difficult? Why?

Question #127

What single activity brings you the most joy in life?

Question #128

What life circumstances cause you the most pain?

Question #129

If you were to take a small step to improve your circumstances in this painful area, what would that look like?

Question #130

If you had to choose between getting in a big blow-up argument that resolved the problem quickly or quietly solving the issue over a matter of days, which one would you prefer, and why?

Question #131

What did you like best about going through the questions in this book with your significant other?

Keeping Love Going

I hope these relationship questions have been enjoyable and that you have gained new insights into the inner world of the person you care about deeply. If so, then congratulations! The goal of this book was to stir up conversations leading to deeper levels of connection, and you have succeeded!

However, don't stop here. Intimacy is an ongoing journey. Stay curious about your loved one, and remember to keep sharing your inner world as well. You can find additional resources for growing your love at: **www.coffeeshopconversations.com**

About the Author

Jed is passionate about helping people live happy, healthy, more connected lives by having better conversations. He is a husband, a father of four girls, a psychology professor, therapist, and a writer.

Jed graduated from Southern California Seminary with a Master of Divinity and returned to complete a second master's degree in psychology. In his free time, Jed enjoys walking on the beach, reading, and spending time with his incredible family.

Continue the Conversation

If you enjoyed this book, please consider leaving a rating and review on Amazon. Because I am a new author, your feedback is a tremendous encouragement and helps books like this one get noticed. It only takes a minute, and every review is much appreciated. Oh, and please feel free to keep in touch too!

Email: jed@coffeeshopconversations.com

Twitter: @jjurchenko

Facebook: Coffee Shop Conversations

More Creative Conversations

Find this book and other books in the
Creative Conversations series on Amazon.

It is never too early or too late to grow
your relationship. Whether you are on your
first date, approaching your golden
anniversary, or somewhere in between, these
creative, Christ-honoring conversation
starters will help you to draw closer together
than ever before.

More Creative Conversations

Deepen your relationship while creating an abundance of happy memories. These creative, insightful, and much-needed conversation starters will help you dive deeper into your relationship and grow in your understanding of each other.

With the overall divorce rate hovering around 50 percent, there is no doubt that marriage can be tricky. This book is for couples who want to defy the odds by building a strong foundation before proclaiming "I do!"

More Creative Conversations

These creative conversation starters will inspire your kids to pause their electronics, grow their social skills, and develop lifelong relationships!

This book is for children and tweens who desire to build face-to-face connections and everyone who wants to help their kids connect in an increasingly disconnected world. Get your kids talking with this activity book the entire family will enjoy.

Made in the USA
Monee, IL
07 November 2019